Exposing the Power of Darkness

DAVID AJAERE

Exposing the Power of Darkness

Copyright © 2013 David Ajaere

All rights reserved. No part of this publication may be reproduced, stored in a cloud or retrieval system, or transmitted, in any form or by any means, electronic, mechanical, photocopying, recording or otherwise, except as expressly permitted by law, without the prior, written permission of the author.

ISBN: 978-0-9927882-0-9

Scripture extracts taken from *Holy Bible (KJV)* by Paul Avery, 2013.

Published by David Ajaere.
Printed in the United Kingdom.

• • •

Website:
www.risingofGodarmy.co.uk

Please give feedback on this book to:
davidajaere@risingofGodarmy.co.uk

Table of Contents

• ✝ •

Introduction 7

Anti-Christ and the Church 13

The Ordained Churches of God 19

Satan's Devices 25

Free from the Power of Darkness 31

How to Break the Power of Darkness 37

Conclusion 43

Introduction

Introduction

• ✟ •

Exposing the power of darkness was revealed to me by God Almighty through God's revelation.

God is light, and in him is no darkness at all.
(1 JOHN 1:5)

Christ shines in the darkness of men's hearts, but men do not understand that it is Christ gently reasoning with them and attempting to reprove them for their evil ways.

But all things that are reproved are made manifest by the light; for whatsoever doth make manifest is light. (EPHESIANS 5:13)

If men believe what God tells them, they believe and love the truth ... but if they deny His reasoning and continue to love their selfish ways, they hate the truth and light which is Christ.

• • •

I was lying in bed, meditating on the word of God, and immediately went into a trance.

God showed me the kingdom of this world and the three major powers that rule and control the world today.

Some of the largest sectors of power were created by Satan and have since become occult centres. I saw that this world's different occult groups are now so widespread that there are few people who don't belong to one of them.

Those who do not serve God in truth and in spirit are like a goat waiting to be slaughtered by an occult group. Their destiny has been stolen from them and used by these occult groups. These people seem unable to function normally in life if they don't belong to an occult group. These secret societies are:

- politics
- the entertainment industry
- various religious groups

Sometimes, these various occult groups clash with each other. They are deceived by Satan and they think that their gods are real, unaware that they are under one master called Satan. God revealed to me that Satan appears to occult leaders as God. Satan gives them evil powers and riches to fulfil his will and undertake his deeds in this world. He appears to them under different names and he sends his satanic fallen angels to appear before them and govern them:

- as god of the sea
- as god of the sun
- as god of the trees and idols

Many ethnic groups still worship these false gods.

Then it was revealed to me that a giant bear and a lion will descend from the sky in the form of the glory of God and appear to all God's army who worship Him in truth and in spirit.

They offer the physical and spiritual power to wage war with the various occults group in this world. When they walk, the earth will shake.

God asked me, "Where would you like to belong?"

I said, "Lord, I want to belong to your lions that wage war against these false prophets and occult leaders."

Immediately, I saw myself cracking jokes in a congregation of people.

God said to me, "Raise my army on this earth."

And I woke up.

I pray in the name of Jesus to all God's army that they have the hunger to receive the power to shake the world, and that they expose and defeat the kingdom of darkness, in Jesus' mighty name. Amen.

• • •

Anti-Christ
and Church
the

Anti-Christ and the Church

• ✝ •

These days there are so many churches. The false pastors and prophets deceive God's people with miracles and signs and wonders in the name of God. They twist the word of God upside down to suit their aims. Don't get me wrong, I'm not against the signs and wonders. But Satan now uses these very tools of God's miracles with his agent, the anti-Christ, to deceive God's people by posing as a true man of God. Brethren, not every pastor that sees visions or claims to be called in the name of God is a true man of God. My Bible says:

Every spirit that confesseth not that Jesus Christ is come in the flesh is not of God: and this is that spirit of antichrist, whereof ye have heard that it should come; and even now already is it in the world.

Ye are of God, little children, and have overcome them: because greater is he that is in you, than he that is in the world. (1 JOHN 4:3-4)

Today, some pastors have sold their soul to the devil in exchange for power. These pastors don't preach salvation. All they preach is their pocket. They encourage people to sow a seed to any ongoing problem they have instead of sharing God's word about that particular problem or situation. They twist the words and teachings of the Bible to suck and empty your pocket in the name of God. They perform magic and tell you everything you would like to hear.

These particular pastors do not promote God's Kingdom. Their entire focus is on expanding their church membership in order to line their own pockets. It's not for the purpose of salvation.

God revealed to me some magicians and herbalists who have converted themselves into suited pastors who pose as God's ordained ministers. Their duty is to turn churches upside down and put fear into its members by appearing to be God's disciple, while at the same time they commit adultery with members of their church in order to control them.

These false pastors can see the blessed one or the ordained man of God who has not even started his ministry or did not yet know he had a calling from God. They will try to use him for his own favour. If they notice that this brother cannot be used, or if he disagrees with them, they will try to use their evil power to put a curse on him. But I tell you, such a curse will not hold, because he whom God has not cursed, no one can curse.

I pray in the name of Jesus, as God Almighty has revealed to me through a vision, to expose the hidden secrets of the devil's devices in this world, and that whoever is under the influence of any false pastor will be set free.

Now, say with me, "I set myself free from every satanic bondage, in Jesus' name. Amen."

• • •

The Ordained Churches of God

The Ordained Churches of God

• ✟ •

In some of the ordained churches of God, the devil has sent his agents to occupy important positions such as usher and leader within the church. Their activities in these churches are to prevent and limit the church's growth. They make sure that the lost sons and daughters of God, from all different walks of life, who are bound up by Satan are not saved. Eventually, God may speak to these lost sons and daughters and direct them to these churches. Or some of them may realise their mistakes and now know the truth that God is the only way. They may then turn from their sinful ways and hunger to serve God.

But these satanic agents make sure that once these lost sons and daughters walk into the church, they are frustrated not to be given a chance to perform or contribute in a different department in that church.

Indeed, the ordained man of God may not even recognise for some time that these are his brethren.

Satan has covered their glory so that no one can recognise the glory of God in their life. I pray in the name of Jesus, whichever devil has covered their glory for whatever reason, that it be uncovered right now, in Jesus' mighty name. Amen.

Put on the whole armour of God, that ye may be able to stand against the wiles of the devil.
(EPHESIANS 6:11)

God now says to all genuine men of God who serve and worship Him in spirit and in truth, to take time to find out what is going on in their local church. Some of these true men of God complain or question why their church is not growing and why the power of God is not moving in their various services.

Today, God is speaking to you of His sons and daughters who were directed to the church but have been rejected by the occult leaders hidden in the name of God. These sons and daughters of God have been sent to you to deliver and help promote the Kingdom of God in this world.

I pray in the name of Jesus, that in every church ordained by God wherever an enemy of God's Kingdom operates, that they be exposed and disgraced, in the mighty name of Jesus our Lord. Amen.

• • •

Satan's Devices

Satan's Devices

In meekness instructing those that oppose themselves; if God peradventure will give them repentance to the acknowledging of the truth; and that they may recover themselves out of the snare of the devil, who are taken captive by him at his will.
(2 TIMOTHY 2:25-26)

There's a category of people in this world ordained by Almighty God born to do great things and to be a blessing to his family and to his generation. Eighty percent of these people are bound in captivity by Satan right from the time they are born. This is why the world is full of evil. Because God's chosen people who are supposed to occupy the most important positions in government and other sectors of power are not recognised and therefore have no influence.

Satan often uses the spirit of divorce and poverty to attack these families. He will use these devices to frustrate and negatively affect a destined child's upbringing. If the child's parents are not prayerful, they will fall wholly to the devices of Satan.

Once Satan launches his devices, there will be a misunderstanding between a husband and his wife and it may lead to divorce. They may think that divorce will solve their problem. They will not know that it is the beginning of their problem and they may not give themselves enough time and patience to work it through. Nor will they commit their problem to Almighty God who is the problem solver without injustice. God says, "I hate divorce."

> *The Pharisees also came unto him, tempting him, and saying unto him, is it lawful for a man to put away his wife for every cause? And Jesus answered and said unto them, Have ye not read, that he which made them at the beginning made them male and female, and said, For this cause shall a man leave his father and mother, and shall cleave to his wife: and they twain shall be one flesh? Wherefore they are no more twain, but one flesh. What therefore God hath joined together, let not man put asunder.* (MATTHEW 19:3-4-5-6)

This problem will automatically extend to the children left without a father. Their mother will try to be both a father and a mother, making it almost impossible to bring up their children in a good manner unless God assists them.

This problem may also lead to poverty because God's glory through the married couple's promise has been broken. The child may lack fatherly love and discipline.

He that spareth his rod hateth his son: but he that loveth him chasteneth him betimes. (PROVERBS 13:24)

As soon as this child becomes a teenager, he or she may be desperate to survive. A girl may become a prostitute in order to live. A boy may pursue illegal activities like thieving, armed robbery, drug dealing or fraud for fast or easy money.

Instead of considering university or a legitimate job, a child may be consumed by the spirit of greed and evil. He or she might exercise all their godly wisdom and talent on evil instead of good things. At that stage, Satan the accuser and deceiver of brethren will temporarily allow them to prosper and will lead them into bondage. They may not fulfil their God-given destiny and that child will keep wallowing in darkness.

But God will not leave them. He will continue knocking in their heart and sending messages for them to repent.

I pray in the name of Jesus that all satanic devices launched against any family and child ordained for greatness are destroyed. In Jesus' mighty name. Amen.

• • •

Free from the Power of Darkness

Free from the Power of Darkness

• ☨ •

The time is fulfilled, and the kingdom of God is at hand: repent ye, and believe the gospel. (MARK 1:15)

Brethren, you can set yourself free from the power of darkness and avoid sin in your life.

Blessed is he whose transgression is forgiven, whose sin is covered. (PSALM 32:1)

Welcome God into your life.

Seek ye first the kingdom of God, and all these things shall be added unto you. (MATTHEW 6:33)

Pray without ceasing.

Call unto me, and I will answer thee, and shew thee great and mighty things, which thou knowest not. (JEREMIAH 33:3)

Sing spiritual songs and make melodies in your heart. Always give thanks to Almighty God for your life.

> *Speaking to yourself in psalms and hymns and spiritual songs, singing and making melody in your heart to the Lord; giving thanks always for all things unto God and the Father in the name of our Lord Jesus Christ.* (EPHESIANS 5:19-20)

Study the word of God. Speak and declare the word of God to everyone in your own world. I mean, in your workplace, your house, your shops, your school, and in all the places you visit every day. When you do this daily the word of God will come alive in your spirit. Your mindset and your character will gradually change and transform you for His glory. You will begin to hear and interact with the Holy Spirit. Your communion with Christ will reach a higher level. These are God's promises to you. The seven gifts of the Holy Spirit will automatically manifest in your life.

> *Follow after charity, and desire spiritual gifts, but rather that ye may prophesy. For he that speaketh in an unknown tongue speaketh not unto men, but unto God: for no man understandeth him; howbeit in the spirit he speaketh mysteries.* (1 CORINTHIANS 14:1-2)

Brethren, I tell you, when you apply all these things in

your life there will be no darkness because the light of God will shine in your life.

•••

How to Break the Power of Darkness

How to Break the Power of Darkness

• ✝ •

He brought them out of darkness and the shadow of death, and brake their bands in sunder. (PSALMS 107:14)

Please offer this prayer with me:

1) In the name of Jesus, by the blood of Jesus, I break and I destroy every satanic covenant in my life.

2) In the name of Jesus, by the blood of Jesus, I break and I destroy every satanic curse in my life and in my family.

3) In the name of Jesus, by the blood of Jesus, I break and I destroy every satanic sin in my life and in my generation.

4) In the name of Jesus, by the blood of Jesus, I break and I scatter every satanic delay and denial in my life.

5) In the name of Jesus, by the blood of Jesus, I break and I destroy every satanic manipulation in my life and in my family.

6) In the name of Jesus, by the blood of Jesus, I break and I destroy every satanic embargo imposed on my success.

7) In the name of Jesus, by the blood of Jesus, I break and I destroy every satanic agent's programme to stop my glory.

8) In the name of Jesus, by the blood of Jesus, I break and I destroy every satanic monitoring agent in my life.

9) In the name of Jesus, by the blood of Jesus, I break and I destroy every satanic gathering against my life.

10) In the name of Jesus, by the blood of Jesus, I break and I destroy every satanic conspiracy in my life.

11) In the name of Jesus, by the blood of Jesus, I break and I destroy every satanic temple that negatively represents my life.

12) In the name of Jesus, by the blood of Jesus, I break and I destroy every generational curse in my life and in my family.

13) In the name of Jesus, by the blood of Jesus, I break and I destroy every satanic hindrance in my life.

14) In the name of Jesus, by the blood of Jesus, I break and I destroy every satanic hindrance in my work and in my business.

15) In the name of Jesus, by the blood of Jesus, I break and I destroy every satanic disease planted in my life and in my family.

・・・

Conclusion

Conclusion

• ✝ •

I wrote this book based on a divine instruction and revelation from God Almighty. I am a successful businessman, and although God sent evangelists and pastors my way to tell me of God's plan in my life, I ignored their messages because I was busy making money. I was involved in several different businesses in Africa until I decided to relocate to the United Kingdom shortly after I married. I wanted to start a family, and my main aim was that my children would benefit from a good education.

But along the way something happened and everything changed. My businesses in Africa began to lose money and I was spending too much in the UK. After seven years, I ran out of money.

I started going to church. I hoped to hear from God and find a solution to my problems. I fasted for one year from six in the morning to six in the evening. That year, God revealed many things to me.

He said, "My son, write this book and raise my army."

I trust that this book will help serve as an eye-opener to what is going on in our world today. I hope that it will help bring deliverance to you and your family, and set you free from satanic schemes and false prophets.

I trust in God that I will start a programme. The theme of this programme is to raise God's army around the world. God has promised to manifest His power and glory through this programme. The sick will be healed. The dead will rise again. We will stand strong together as God's voice, and we will stand up against the principality and rulers of darkness in this world.

...

If you feel that God is calling you

to be a supporter or a participant
of this vision, write to me at:
davidajaere@risingofGodarmy.co.uk

Say, "David Ajaere, I am
in support of God's vision
in your life."

www.ingramcontent.com/pod-product-compliance
Lightning Source LLC
Chambersburg PA
CBHW032053290426
44110CB00012B/1062